PELICAN

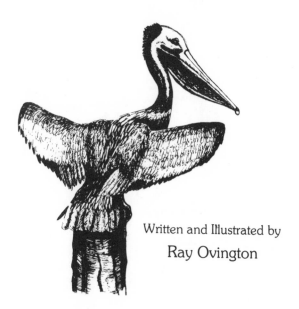

Written and Illustrated by

Ray Ovington

GREAT**OUTDOORS**

PUBLISHING CO.

4747 TWENTY-EIGHTH STREET NORTH   ST. PETERSBURG, FLORIDA 33714

ISBN #0-8200-0905-9

ABOUT THE AUTHOR

Ray Ovington is an old-timer in the writing and illustrating field, known for his books on nature, wildlife and outdoor recreation. His WILDLIFE ILLUSTRATED, BIRDS OF PREY, and GAME BIRDS are popular and academically-accepted books of reference and enjoyment. Living as he does in Ormond Beach, Florida, he frequents the beach often and declares that his favorite bird is the Pelican, "a flier extraordinary, a comedian, a graceful thing, and a friend of fishermen and surfers and vacationers."

"But," he says, "few people know very much about the Pelican except what they see." That's the 'why' of this little book: to acquaint the public with the interesting and fascinating facts about this unique bird of our ocean shorelines and rivers. Like the many water birds native and migrant to Florida, the Pelican deserves much attention for what he is and for what we can do for him in the way of protection.

TABLE OF CONTENTS

The Brown Pelican Has a Special Name   6 - 7

A Bird O' Th' Saouth — Suh!   8

Pelicans On The Wing   10 - 11

Glide And Sail With Grace   12 - 13

And They Like To Perform   14 - 15

But They Best Like To Dive   16 - 17

And Come Up With A Fish   18 - 19

To Take Home To Their Nest   20 - 21

And Feed It To Their Young 'Uns   22 - 23

That Grow Into Big Happy Birds   24 - 25

And Will Join Their Parents   26 - 27

To Parade Like Dancers For You   28 - 29

Cousins and Relatives   30 - 31

Bibliography   32

THE BROWN PELICAN

HAS A SPECIAL NAME

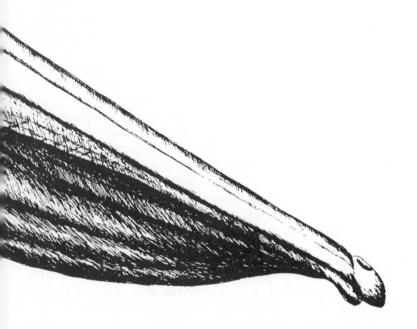

Pelecanus occidentalis occidentalis
(Latin, pecking bird; Latin, western)

A BIRD O' TH'
SAOUTH — SUH!

He can be seen in a broad area encompassing the far-flung jewels of the Florida Keys, the Carolinas along the Atlantic Coast, and westward to Louisiana, Texas and Mexico on the Gulf. The Eastern Brown Pelican claims this all as his home, sharing its warm and friendly climate with other members of his immediate biological Order of Pelicaniformes, or totipalmate swimmers. The White Pelican is next of kin, with the Tropic Bird, Gannet, the four Cormorants, Darters, or Water Turkeys, and Man-o'-war Birds. Also sharing his waterways and flight lanes are numerous other birds such as the terns, gulls, snipes, herons and, in fact, anything that can fly, wade, swim or waddle. Look for him from your motel window overseeing the vast expanse of the beach. He and a flight formation of family and friends will often sail by your balcony almost close enough to touch. Note how they undulate in close formation, gliding all at once — as many as fifteen or twenty, with their wings stretched to an identical glide position. See them overhead when you are surfing; they dip by with wing tips almost brushing the foamy surface. Watch them hover and ride the wind a bit off-shore, hoping to discover a school of mullet or menhaden being gobbled up by jacks, mackerel or other game fish. They'll dive and cause a white flash amidst the white bodies of the gulls. You'll see a proud pelican when he gulps down his prize and sits and rides on the surface for a few minutes before rising again to search out other unfortunates that have been attacked by underwater assailants. He's big, massive, powerful!

A bird of grace once airborne or when gliding and sailing, the pelican is an awkward walker since his feet and legs are set so far back on his frame. He knows he cannot have everything and is thankful for his flight and swimming abilities due to his wide and long, powerful wings and oversize webbed feet. No one knows just why the pelican has such a long bill and its accompanying pouch. Gulls and terns don't need one to catch fish and he doesn't need it to carry his catch.

The Eastern Brown Pelican ranges also into California and southern Oregon and is a bit smaller than the White Pelican and much more common. The Brown's body measures from forty-five to fifty-four inches long, with long slender tail, extra thick and heavy legs and large webbed feet, and a neck as long as his body. His head is large and round and when he flies, his head settles back on his curved neck and his long bill points straight out, forward. He does not extend his neck and head in the manner of some of the waterfowl such as ducks and geese. Wingspan is from eighty to eighty-five inches with long, fingerlike flight feathers that flex under the pressure of his powerful beats on the air.

The White Pelican is a bit larger, with a body length reaching out to seventy inches and wingspan of some eight to ten feet. The White is often found in company with the Brown variety but its range is extended on the Pacific Coast to as far north as British Columbia.

While Pelicans range constantly over their territory, they are not a migrating bird in the true sense of that term, preferring to base their nesting operation to one particular spot or area and ranging about from there as far as a day's flight will take them. Unless disturbed by pollution or destruction of their nesting sites by real estate operators, too much boat traffic or a devastating hurricane, they and their successors will stay at home for generations.

PELICANS ON

The wing flight pattern as shown here is a synchronized routine of flight that makes aerodynamic designers wonder. By an instinctive sensitivity to the wind and its subtle currents, the Pelican seems to exhibit a most efficient motive power to keep his big bulk and heavy weight aloft on the wind, sometimes for many minutes without moving a feather. It is most interesting to watch a line or 'V' formation of Pelicans as they parade down the beach, some hundred feet above the sand. They'll all be flapping their wings for a short spell and then, as if the guide bird gave a signal, they all glide. A closer look at their formation and the way they seem to move into invisible pathways reveals that the birds take advantage of the slightest currents to buoy them up. Off over the ocean while looking for wounded fish or schools of mullet, they will sail sometimes in wide circles, not unlike those of the vulture or wheeling sea gull.

THE WING

The wings of the Pelican are long in the manner of vultures and much wider than those of the common herring gull or tern. Their "fingers", or flight feathers, are long and stiff but seem to bend in the wind under pressure when the need arises. In order to stop quickly, descend or ascend, their "flaps", or secondary feathers, act respectively as brakes or accelerators, aided by their extra strong and power-driven wing beats. Even though they are heavy birds, their weight seems to be well compensated for by their wings and tail. Their long neck is constantly curved back over their shoulders and their head sits on top, with bill forward unless they are looking from side to side in search of fish. They will often fly by and close to surfers and if you look closely they seem to turn their heads toward the humans floating on their boards as if to try to strike up an acquaintance.

GLIDE AND SAIL

WITH GRACE

AND THEY LIKE

One would ordinarily expect to see gulls hovering and standing near the bait dock on the poles and even sometimes the masts of ships. But more often in the South, the Pelican has taken over this close and intriguing relationship with man. Pelicans are bolder, or perhaps more trusting, than the flighty gull, for they become very tame and will quite often take a fresh bit of fish right from the hand. Most marinas have their resident Pelicans standing on the guide posts, or where bait is displayed or fish cleaned. These mascots will waddle up the pier planks to within a few feet and sit there with shining eyes and a laughable countenance, waiting for you to feed them. In some instances they will be aggressive enough to approach you and grab fish right from your bucket or hand. Many of the commercial fishermen and charter boat captains tell stories of Pelicans that have been friends of theirs for many years, even bringing their new young birds to the pier to cadge a handout.

TO PERFORM

You'll often see these birds, either singly or in clusters, perched atop one of the harbor buoys, rocking back and forth if the current is bobbing the buoy about. They seem to enjoy the act and as you ride by in the boat they will all look toward you as if asking for applause. They'll stick there unless you come by too close, too fast. Awkward when on shore or anchored down to the earth, they still exhibit a kind of acrobatic grace. Even when grooming their feathers they present quite a show: stretching their wings, spreading their tail feathers, while massaging their entire body with their long bill, being experts at extricating fatty fluid at the base of their tail and spreading the water-proofing substance over all their feathers. This ritual goes on several times a day, much in the manner of tabby cats who are continually grooming and preening themselves. Their instinct tells them that their buoyancy on the water depends on this waterproofing.

BUT THEY BEST

Pelicans are strictly fish eaters, preferring live mullet and menhaden or other small fish that have been driven to the surface by bigger fish that feed on the schools. They know where and when the mullet school together in the shallows or when, on the outgoing tide, they move in a mass out toward the inlet or bay. During the fall months when the mullet are migrating in long lines down the beach, just beyond the breakers, they will be found hovering above them and diving constantly with great accuracy. They seldom miss.

Watch closely when they dive and you'll see quite a programmed routine that is almost letter-perfect, despite the huge size and seemingly awkward body that presents itself to the uneducated eye. While most sea birds simply fold their wings and dive in, the Pelican has to follow a procedure lest he destroy himself because of the terrific thrust his weight produces on fall.

At the start of the downward plunge, he closes his wings partly and curves his neck so the head is close to the shoulders. Just before contact with the water the wings are extended behind by a quick, short stroke and then he turns his body so that he is actually upside down when he strikes the water and at an angle of about seventy degrees. At that moment he straightens out his neck and the bill enters the water with the pouch upside down — the force of the dive opens the pouch to its full capacity. Then he pops up to the surface into a sitting position with the bill closed and pointed down so that the water drains out of the pouch through special holes. Once the water is removed the bird raises his bill and swallows the fish. He does not use the pouch to carry the loot as is done by other species.

16

LIKE TO DIVE

AND COME UP

WITH A FISH

It is quite a sight to see Pelicans bugging the schools of mullet in the shallows. They'll be flying low to the water, sometimes two or three or more at a time. They'll purposely wing their way over a shallows seen to contain a school of mullet. At the sight of their wings the mullet will jump and splash and scatter in a flash of spray that can cover as much as a fifty foot circle. The Pelicans will merely look down at them and, if low enough, touch their bills to the water. Farther down the shallow they'll buzz another school and then, as if at a signal, all will fly up into the air and return from whence they came, to repeat the performance all over again.

But the most triumphant display of their talents is when they rise from the water having swallowed their fish. There is something registering happiness or accomplishment in the character of the wingbeat and the angle of the head that shows the world that they are real experts at their trade.

Birds under accurate observation have been checked at catching and carrying a dozen or more small mullet at one hunting expedition. With this kind of cargo they are much heavier and thus require a stronger and quicker wingbeat to stay aloft. Their direction is also limited from a lot of wheeling and dealing with the wind. They fly much like our transport planes . . . no fooling around . . . straight to where they are going to alight in order to digest their meal.

When the birds are caring and feeding a nest of little ones, they will often catch just a few fish, preferring to let the meal partially digest so that they can return to the nest with a prepared meal for those ever-hungry maws. It has been a long exercise, perhaps in order to secure the needed nourishment and before returning to the nest they will be seen floating and paddling in an out-of-the-surf-and-wind location where they'll join other parents to discuss the problems of their lives. After a while, rested and with the meal inside digested to the correct amount they'll return to the nest, sometimes a long flight.

TO TAKE HOME

TO THEIR NEST

Since there are no cliffs or protective coves and hidden places along the flat shoreline of Florida or any of the coastline all the way to Mexico, the Pelican is forced to build its nest virtually in the open. They usually select a deep and thick section of mangrove, if in the southern part of Florida, as far from the beaten path of boats and fishermen as they can. find. The ground is usually a bit higher, built up of sand or gravelly base, with thick mangroves and palms and other greenery that can survive at tide level. Near the mouths of rivers the water may be brackish. Here they form rookeries of sometimes hundreds of birds, such as found at Pelican Island in south Florida. There is also a small pelican island at Daytona Beach, where the birds nest in company with many other varieties of sea birds. House cats and rattle-snakes take their toll of the young, but somehow a strong breed of sea birds persists. Where mangroves do not occur they build in what bushes there are and sometimes make their homes in open gravel and driftwood. But they call it home and an eager set of mouths is always hungry. They generally have only one clutch of eggs per year, though at times they may have two. Two, three or sometimes four very white eggs, slightly larger than the extra-large chicken egg, are laid and well cared for by both parents.

AND FEED IT

TO THEIR YOUNG 'UNS

THAT GROW INTO

The birds take turns sitting on the eggs to keep them warm while the other parent goes off in search of a meal. By watching the nest it is possible to see father, for example, bringing home fish and giving it to mother so she can remain on the nest. At other times, as father flies in mother will take off to find her own adventure. The parents are held down to family duties, but it is surprising to watch them exercise with the clan, forming great flights of as many as thirty birds merely to go for an afternoon soar up and down the beach. They seem to have rendezvous points where the birds congregate, starting sometimes from one bird. They will circle around high up, as a signal for others to join them. Soon the flotilla parades before the admiring audience in the seaside motels. Afterwards they disperse for the fishing duties and return to the nest with enough for everybody.

The little ones are hatched with no feathers save a very thin covering of grayish-white fuzz. And they are subject to drafts even then and are kept well covered by the tremendous wings of their parents. Soon, after the first feathers appear, they become active in the nest, flexing their webbed feet, trying to learn to walk. Then they begin to exercise their wings and learn to hold up the large head and beak on a squiggly neck. They are fed constantly, sometimes as many as six times a day, for their growth requires a total of one hundred and fifty pounds of food. This means much hunting and diving by both parents to keep the seemingly endless routine ever going.

BIG HAPPY BIRDS

HIS BEAK CAN HOLD MORE THAN HIS BELLY CAN! CAN!

AND WILL JOIN

THEIR PARENTS

If the nest is high up in the mangroves, the fledglings are taught first to fly, since they will have to reach the water by their wings. The parents stand on a branch to one side of the nest and the inquisitive and admiring young birds mimic their wing movements. Sometimes both parents are seen by the nest waving their wings and then stopping while the little ones copy their movements. Sometimes the young ones stumble and flop back into the nest. The parents are ever mindful of their clumsiness and guard against a steep fall to the ground and its attendant dangers from predators. Without constant parental attendance, the little ones would probably wander off and get lost amidst the other birds of the rookery. When the young are able to lift off for a split second and regain their balance, they are almost ready for full flight. Only when the feathers have grown out to the required maturity and length will the parents allow them to wing and step lightly from branch to branch.

Then the big day comes when they take their first solo flight. From then on, with guidance from mother and father, they are aloft for good. Taught to land and take off from the water, their next instruction must be to enable them to catch their own food. They leave the nest in five weeks. In three years, the birds are fully matured.

TO PARADE LIKE

They will now accompany their parents to the nearby lagoon where the mullet are comparatively easy to spot from the air. They are also taught not to dive into very shallow water lest they crack up their bills and break their wings. Watching the parental guidance in the lesson of diving is a sight to remember. Quite often, the parent bird will intercept the young one if he is not diving quite properly. It is amazing how few birds ever become damaged in this most difficult assignment. They come by the basic routine naturally, since their forebears had been doing the same thing for perhaps millions of years. But the details still have to be learned. In a few days, the parents will troop the little ones, now actually almost as big as they are, off to the deeper water where they'll float them on ocean waves and strong currents. The next and important lesson is that of rendezvousing with the older birds to learn the stage performances of unison gliding and winging that are a traditional part of their flying art so much appreciated by the human observers below. It is usually quite easy to spot the beginners in the chorus line, but soon they mimic their parents and the older ones and become full fledged performers, adding grace and character to the shoreline and waterways.

DANCERS FOR YOU

POISON . . . is their worst enemy. It can be in the form of spilled oil from careless ship owners. This oil slick covers the water, adheres to the birds' feathers so they cannot fly, and so they succumb to a terrible death. Other forms of industrial wastes, plastic rings from six-packs, fishing line, sewage from boats and shore communities and, worst of all, insecticide residues that have been washed into the waterways kill many birds each year. Also, their food supply of fresh and good fish being poisoned will infect them by secondary exposure.

Real estate development, too much boat traffic near their nests and constant disturbance of their rookeries have endangered their lives and livelihood. They then must pick up and move to another location. Fortunately, they have not been shot for their food value or for their feathers. Only target-hungry people have shot them for sport. They are now fully protected by law from such wanton killing, but their real estate is still ruinable by man.

The Pelican, then, is a barometer of the times. When he lives and prospers and multiplies to give us a refreshing sight of his presence among us, all is well. When the time comes when he becomes only a legend among us, we too may shortly become a part of that very same legend. When the Pelican disappears, after having thrived for so many millions of years, it will indicate something drastically wrong with our "dominion over" the land.

THEY NEED PROTECTION!

29

IN FLORIDA IT'S THE BIG BROWN PELICAN

WHITE PELICAN, *Pelecanus erythrorhynchos*

Body length, fifty-four inches to seventy-two inches; wingspan eight feet to ten feet. Color, white, with black wing-tips and long, yellow bill and yellow pouch. Short legs and big, grayish webbed feet.

Breeds in colonies on islands and inland lakes on the ground or in the mangroves and other bushes and undergrowth. Sometimes builds nest in bare sand. Two to five eggs are laid, colored chalky white. Range is from central British Columbia and Great Slave Lake south to central Manitoba, southern Texas and southern California, the Gulf States and Florida, both coasts of Mexico and as far south as Panama.

YELLOW-BILLED TROPIC-BIRD, *Phaeton lepturus catesbyi*

Bird length from thirty inches to thirty-two inches with a twenty inch tail, wingspread from thirty-four inches to thirty-nine inches. Color is all white except for lesser wing coverts and tertials, partly black primaries and a black mark before and through the eye. Two central tail feathers are very long. Flight pattern is quick and pigeon-like. Range is from Bermuda and West Indies and Bahamas south to Florida and Brazil.

GANNET, *Moris bassana*

Length of body from thirty-three inches to forty inches with wingspread about seventy inches. Adult is white with black wingtips, in flight wingtips are very sharp. Head and tail both pointed. They dive for fish and go deep under the surface. Breed on sea cliffs or islands in remote areas. Two eggs are laid, bluish white. Range is from the St. Lawrence River and southern Newfoundland and Europe, to Florida and the Gulf of Mexico.

MAN O' WAR BIRD, *Fregata magnificens*

Known as the Frigate Bird, its length is from thirty-eight inches to forty-two inches, with a wingspan of seven feet to eight feet. Color, black. Breeds in colonies. One egg is laid that is white in color. Range is southern States, Bahamas and Central America.

AND ALL AROUND THE WORLD ARE HIS COUSINS

EUROPEAN CORMORANT, *Phalacrocorax carbo carbo*

Body length from thirty-four inches to forty inches with wingspread about five feet. Adult bronze-blackish, with small white patch on throat and flanks. Breeds in colonies on cliffs, islands and in mangroves with other water birds. Nest of sticks and seaweed. Lays four to six eggs, chalky bluish-white color. Range is from western Greenland and Cumberland Sound to Florida. A long-necked bird who flies with neck stretched out in front, not gathered up like the herons and pelicans.

DOUBLE-CRESTED CORMORANT, *Phalacrocorax auritus auritus*

Smaller than the European Cormorant, with body length from twenty-nine inches to thirty-five inches, wingspan from fifty inches to fifty-three inches. Two crests of feathers on the head, gray colored. Rest of bird is bronze-black, sometimes with a greenish highlight. Flies with neck and head stretched out in front. Breeding similar to the European variety as is its range.

FLORIDA CORMORANT, *Phalacrocorax auritus floridanus*

Known as the Water Turkey in Florida, it is slightly smaller than the Double-Crested Cormorant with similar habits and distribution. Almost identical in color and shape and habits to the Double-Crested.

MEXICAN CORMORANT, *Phalacrocorax olivaceus mexicanus*

Smaller than the Double-Crested variety, with similar plumage and nesting and breeding habits. Southern resident; rarely found

WATER TURKEY, *Anhinga anhinga*

Length from thirty-four inches to thirty-six inches, with a wingspan of forty-four inches. Resembles the Cormorant but with longer, more slender neck held out straight in flight. Blackish-brown color, with greenish highlights. Breeding habits similar to Cormorants. Range from southern California to Florida and southern Gulf States.

BIBLIOGRAPHY AND SUGGESTED REFERENCES

AUDUBON, JOHN J. Birds of America. New York: Macmillan Co., 1976.

AUSTIN, OLIVER L., JR. Families of Birds. New York: Golden Press, 1971.

BARREUL, E. THOMAS. Birds of the World. London: Oxford Univ. Press, 1973.

FICHTER, GEORGE S. Birds of Florida. E. A. Seeman Press, 1972.

FORBUSH, EDW. H. Natural History of American Birds. John May Co., 1956

GUILLIARD, E. THOMAS. Living Birds of the World. New York: Doubleday, 1958.

LAYCOCK, GEORGE. The Pelicans. New York: Natural History Press.

LONGSTREET, RUPERT J. Birds in Florida. Miami: Trend House, 1969.

MAY, CHARLES P. Book of American Birds. New York: St. Martin, 1967.

PETERSON, ROGER TORY. Field Guide to the Birds. Boston: Houghton-Mifflin.